Grammar Made Easy

for Infants

Book 1

By

Cheryl .M. Greenidge

This book is dedicated to the staff and students of

the St. Martins-Mangrove Primary School which is

situated in St. Martin's, St. Philip, Barbados.

Book 1

First edition 2015

Cover design by Todd Forde
Back cover photo: Students of St. Martin's-Mangrove Primary
Edited by E. Jerome Davis
Published by Cheryl .M. Greenidge

ISBN   10: 1514613875

ISBN   13: 978-1514613870

ABOUT THE AUTHOR

Cheryl Greenidge attended St. Martins Girl's School, the Princess Margaret Secondary School and the Barbados Community College. In 1988, she started her career as a primary school teacher. In 1997, she enrolled at the Erdiston Teacher's Training College where she completed her Diploma in Education. In 2005, Cheryl was made Early Childhood Coordinator at the St. Martin's - Mangrove Primary School. Cheryl's years of experience in the infants' department have greatly assisted her in compiling the material for this book. She is the author of 'Word Building for Infants', 'A Spelling and Reading Aid for Beginners' and 'Grammar Made Easy for Infants' – Books 2, 3 and 4.

CONTENTS

PREFACE

The call by local educators for more Barbadian teachers to publish their work has encouraged me to publish my second book entitled "Grammar Made Easy for Infants".

"Grammar Made Easy for Infants" introduces the concepts of **a** and **an**, **nouns**, **singular** and **plural**, **am**, **is** and **are**, and **capital letters**.

Every effort has been made to present the concepts in a simple but interesting manner. The many activities are presented in a variety of ways in order to reinforce the concepts.

A feature of the text is the inclusion of Barbadian references which help to create that connection between child and activity.

"Grammar Made Easy for Infants" although specially designed for the 5 – 7 age group, may be helpful to older children who have not mastered the concepts presented.

Section 1

Vowels

a and an

✿ Write the missing letter for the pictures.

a, e, i, o, u

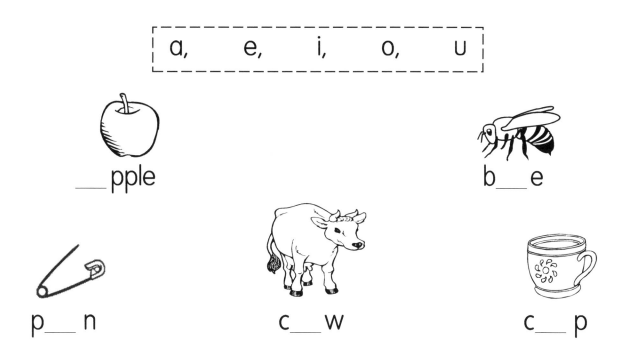

__pple

b__e

p__n

c__w

c__p

✿ The letters a, e, i, o, u are called vowels.
Circle the vowels in the clouds.

e d a z o

n u g e f

i v p u r

k a i t o

✤ Write one vowel in each flower.

✤ Colour the kite if the word begins with a vowel.

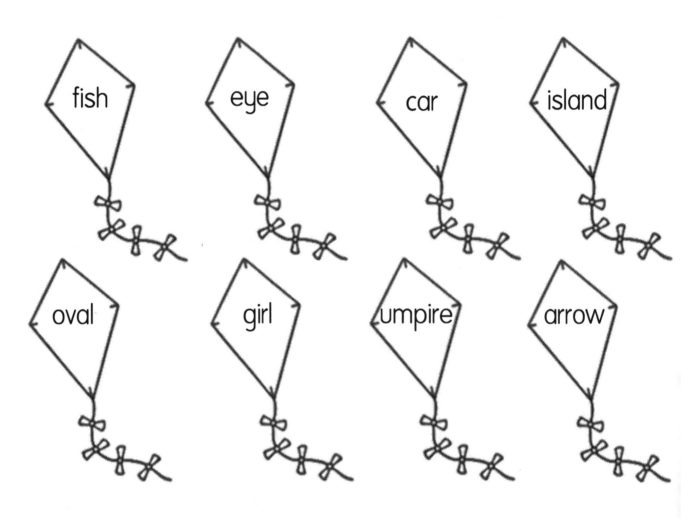

fish   eye   car   island

oval   girl   umpire   arrow

✿ Circle the words which begin with a vowel.

dog   igloo   van   sun   uncle

apple   pig   orange   bun

egg   chair   aunt

✿ Now write the words which you circled in the 'an' box. Write the other words in the 'a' box.

an	a
_____	_____
_____	_____
_____	_____
_____	_____
_____	_____
_____	_____

✿ We write 'an' before most words which begin with a vowel. Write 'an' before the words below.

_____ egg   _____ owl   _____ uncle

_____ oven   _____ apple   _____ ice cream

_____ ankle   _____ ear   _____ umbrella

✿ We write 'a' before most words which do not begin with a vowel. Write 'a' before the words below.

_____ cat   _____ wall   _____ flag

_____ ship   _____ ball   _____ tree

✿ **Circle the correct word in the brackets.**

(a   an) house   (a   an) insect

(a   an) oven   (a   an) ackee

(a   an) earring   (a   an) duck

✿ **Circle the correct word in the brackets.**

1. He has (a   an) bat.

2. That is (a   an) ugly picture.

3. May I have (a   an) snack?

4. We saw (a   an) ape at the zoo.

5. Barbados is (a   an) island.

❀ Write 'a' or 'an' before these words.

_____ book   _____ orange   _____ door

_____ eye   _____ aunt   _____ pencil

_____ mat   _____ rubber   _____ octopus

❀ Write 'a' or 'an' in the spaces.

1. He has _____ bat.

2. Did you see _____ alligator in the water?

3. I will buy _____ ice cream.

4. Have _____ good day.

5. She ate _____ apple and _____ banana.

Section 2

Nouns

- things
- animals
- persons
- places

✿ Match these things to their naming words.

hat

fan

pen

boat

bell

cup

✿ **Write the naming words for these things.**

pan	sun	net	pot	fire
bat	well	jet	banana	

_____   _____   _____

_____   _____   _____

_____   _____   _____

✿ Words which name things are called naming words or nouns. Circle the noun in each box.

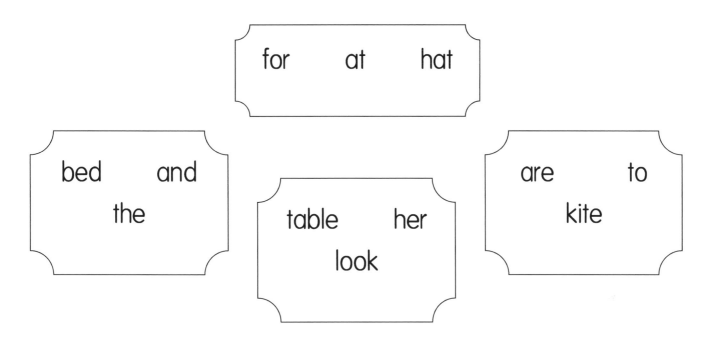

for   at   hat

bed   and
    the

table   her
    look

are   to
    kite

✿ In the sentences, circle the nouns which name <u>things</u>.

1. Look at the little box.

2. The car is red.

3. Here is my book.

4. Run to the tree.

5. She has a big bag.

6. This ball is mine.

✿ Write the nouns (things) below in suitable cans.

sun   bell   smoke

book   cake   radio   gas

pen   moon   ham

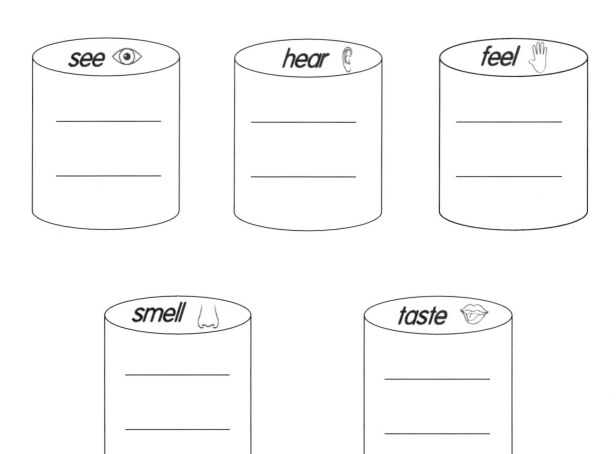

✿ Words which name animals are called naming words or nouns. Write the names of these animals.

| fish | pig | goat | duck |

_____   _____   _____   _____

✿ Write these nouns (animals) in the correct boxes.

| cat | bird | swan | eel | hen |
| whale | sheep | dog | shark |

Live in the Sea	Can Fly	Have Four Legs
_____	_____	_____
_____	_____	_____
_____	_____	_____

✤ **Circle the naming word (noun) in each box.**

write	bird	put

fox	my	this

come	all	bear

chick	it	see

for	ant	look

✤ **In the sentences, circle the nouns which name <u>animals.</u>**

1. Look at the little rabbit.

2. The monkey is swinging.

3. Did you see my cat?

4. The cow is brown.

5. She has a big dog.

❀ Words which name persons are called naming words or nouns. Write the names of these persons.

| teacher | boy | daddy | police |

Nouns
things animals
people places

_____   _____   _____   _____

❀ Write these nouns (persons) in the correct boxes.

boy   mummy   girl   daddy   baby   grandma

adult

_____
_____
_____

child

_____
_____
_____

✤ **Circle the naming word (noun) in each box.**

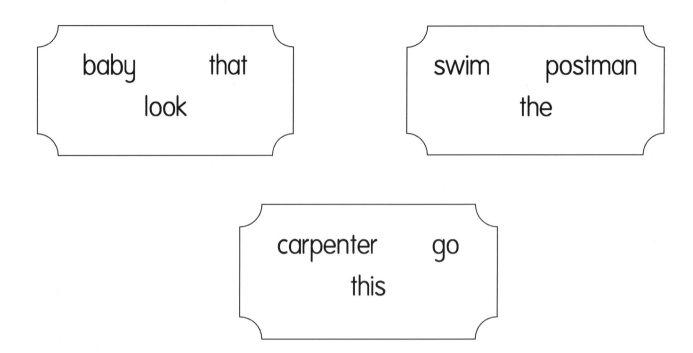

baby   that   look

swim   postman   the

carpenter   go   this

✤ **In the sentences, circle the nouns which name <u>persons.</u>**

1. The boys are playing.

2. The maid is cleaning.

3. Is he your granddad?

4. The chef is cooking.

5. Are the girls washing?

✿ Words which name places are called naming words or nouns. Write the names of these places.

| bathroom | mall | garden | park |

_____   _____   _____   _____

✿ Circle the noun (place) in each box.

| shop   the   talk |

| school   of   then |

| play   in   Bridgetown |

| here   library   jump |

| are   home   did |

19

✿ Complete each sentence with the correct noun.

beach

bedroom

supermarket

church

office

1. The baby sleeps in the _____.

2. Daddy works in an _____.

3. The children play on the _____.

4. Mummy shops at the _____.

5. Grandma likes going to _____.

✿ Words which name animals, persons, places and things are called nouns. Write these nouns in the correct boxes.

daddy	market	town	goat	runner	tablet
flower	chip	park	lizard	fly	driver

Animal

_____

_____

_____

Person

_____

_____

_____

Place

_____

_____

_____

Thing

_____

_____

_____

✵ **Circle the nouns in the sentences.**

Example: The (cat) is fat.

1. My cup is little.

2. Look at the tree.

3. The girl is going to school.

4. Is the beach far away?

5. A bird is on the wall.

6. An apple is on the table.

7. My book is in my bag.

8. Some children are on the pasture.

9. Water is in the well.

Section 3

Plurals

- most nouns
- nouns ending in 'ch'
- nouns ending in 'sh'
- nouns ending in 's'
- nouns ending in 'ss'
- nouns ending in 'x'
- irregular nouns

✿ We add 's' to most nouns to make them more than one. Make these nouns more than one.

dog

ball

car

dogs

girl

mill

tree

cow

boat

chair

✤ Make these nouns more than one.

One   More Than One

wall   _____

hen   _____

cat   _____

van   _____

pig   _____

mat   _____

❀ Make these nouns more than one.

rat

bird

cup

_____   _____   _____

❀ Make the noun in brackets more than one.
Write it in the space.

1. The boy eats two _____. (bun)

2. The hen has many _____. (egg)

3. Do you have the _____? (ball)

4. Mummy buys some _____. (pill)

5. Some _____ are in the pen. (pig)

✤ Write the nouns in the correct boxes.

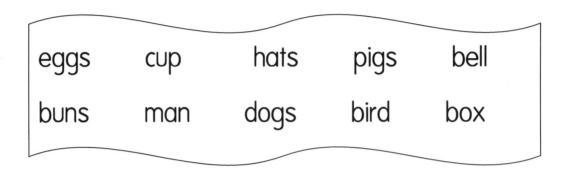

eggs   cup   hats   pigs   bell

buns   man   dogs   bird   box

More Than One

One

✿ Read the words for the pictures. Circle the letters that make the words similar.

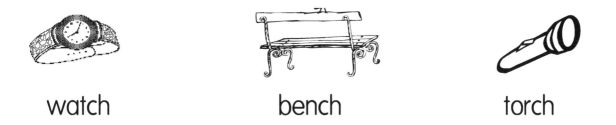

watch   bench   torch

✿ Underline the nouns which end with 'ch'. Then write them in the box.

match	hook	latch	table	beach
cheese	torch	boat	church	chair
branch	shoe	peach	road	ostrich

_____   _____

_____   _____

_____   _____

_____   _____

✿ We add 'es' to nouns which end with 'ch' to make them more than one. Make these nouns more than one.

_____   _____   _____

✿ Make these nouns more than one.

One	More Than One
latch	_____
torch	_____
stitch	_____
hutch	_____
bunch	_____
cockroach	_____

❀ Make these nouns more than one.

branch

church

sandwich

_____   _____   _____

❀ Make the noun in brackets more than one.
Write it in the space.

1. Do not play with _____. (match)

2. Will you pack the _____? (lunch)

3. The _____ are new. (watch)

4. The man walks with _____. (crutch)

5. We sat on the _____. (bench)

31

✿ Read the words for the pictures. Circle the letters that make the words similar.

brush   fish   sash

✿ Underline the nouns which end with 'sh'. Then write them in the box.

dish	coach	sash	flag	bush
house	brush	shoe	flash	window
fish	roof	splash	shirt	crash

_____   _____

_____   _____

_____   _____

_____   _____

❀ We add 'es' to nouns which end with 'sh' to make
them more than one. Make these nouns more than one.

| dish | eyelash | flash |

_____   _____   _____

❀ Make these nouns more than one.

One   More Than One

lash   _____

splash   _____

wish   _____

dash   _____

crash   _____

✿ Make these nouns more than one.

| sash | toothbrush | fish |

_____ _____ _____

✿ Make the noun in brackets more than one.
Write it in the space.

1. Put the _____ in the sink. (dish)

2. Mummy bought two _____. (brush)

3. We saw many _____ in the sky. (flash)

4. Her _____ are long. (eyelash)

5. Did he hit the ball into the _____? (bush)

✿ **Match the nouns to the correct boxes to show how we make them more than one.**

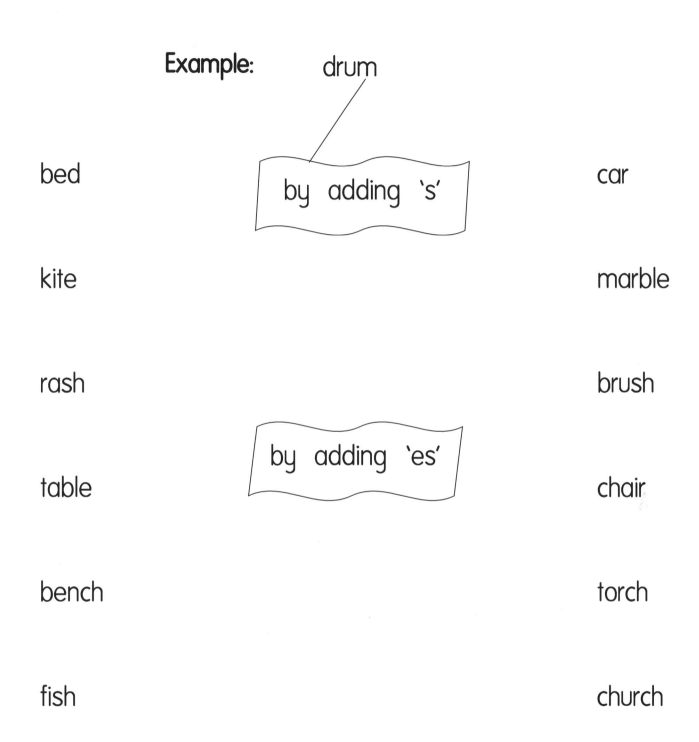

Example: drum

bed

kite

rash

table

bench

fish

by adding 's'

by adding 'es'

car

marble

brush

chair

torch

church

✿ Make these nouns more than one.

chair___   flash___   house___   peach___

wish___   beach___   crash___   clock___

✿ Make the noun in brackets one. Write it in the space.

1. The _____ is on the table. (cakes)

2. Daddy caught a _____ . (fishes)

3. A _____ is in the sea. (boats)

4. The man pulls the _____ . (nets)

5. Did you wash the _____ ? (dishes)

✿ **Make the noun in brackets more than one.**
Write it in the space.

1. May I have my _____? (pencil)

2. The girls put on their_____. (sash)

3. Here are the _____. (book)

4. Did he find the ball in the _____? bush)

5. The _____ were lit. (torch)

6. The rabbits are in the _____. (hutch)

7. Some _____ live in the tree. (bird)

8. The West Indies won two _____? (match)

9. Daddy has new paint _____. (brush)

✿ Read the words for the pictures. Circle the letter that makes the words similar.

lens   bus   atlas

✿ Underline the nouns which end with 's' and write them in the box.

rock   bus   key   peach   canvas

gas   skirt   boat   atlas   shoe

_____   _____

_____   _____

✤ Read the words for the pictures. Circle the letters that make the words similar.

princess   cross   glass

✤ Underline the nouns which end with 'ss' and write them in the box.

grass	rain	tea	guess	peach
frog	soap	kiss	house	press
salt	class	boat	dress	book

_____   _____

_____   _____

_____   _____

✤ We add 'es' to nouns which end with 's' and 'ss' to make them more than one. Make these nouns more than one.

dress

bus

class

_____ _____ _____

✤ Make these nouns more than one.

One	More Than One
grass	_____
atlas	_____
press	_____
gas	_____
boss	_____

✿ **Make the noun in brackets more than one. Write it in the space.**

1. I have two new _____ (dress).

2. The _____ are going to Bridgetown. (bus)

3. I gave daddy many _____. (kiss)

4. Did she break the _____? (glass)

5. Look for the _____ in the cupboard. (lens)

✿ **Make the noun in brackets one. Write it in the space.**

1. She is a pretty _____. (princesses)

2. Are the boys in the _____? (classes)

3. That _____ came from Farley Hill. (buses)

4. A _____ is on the church. (crosses)

✤ Read the words for the pictures. Circle the letter that makes the words similar.

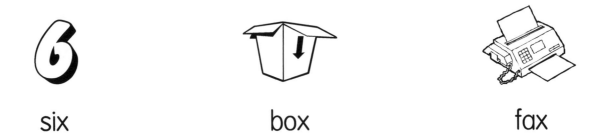

six   box   fax

✤ Underline the nouns which end with 'x' and write them in the box.

fax	text	six	bus	far
tan	fox	rake	sky	pox
ski	sax	bed	wax	lot

_____   _____

_____   _____

_____   _____

✼ We add 'es' to most nouns which end with 'x' to make them more than one. Make these nouns more than one.

| sax | fox | tax |

_____   _____   _____

✼ Make these nouns more than one.

One	More Than One
six	_____
box	_____
fax	_____
mix	_____
wax	_____

❀ **Make the noun in the brackets more than one. Write it in the space.**

1. Mummy paid her ____________. (tax)
2. The men will paint the ____________. (box)
3. Many ____________ were in the den. (fox)
4. Sobers hit six ____________ in one over. (six)

❀ **Make the noun in the brackets one. Write it in the space.**

1. Five plus one makes ____________. (sixes)
2. She has one ____________. (boxes)
3. The ____________ ate the hen. (foxes)
4. Daddy pays road ____________. (taxes)

✿ Match the nouns to the correct boxes to show how we make them more than one.

Example:

door

house

box

road

lens

cross

apple

by adding 's'

by adding 'es'

van

tablet

dish

cake

atlas

church

✿ Colour the book if the noun means many (more than one).

❀ Some nouns change to become many (more than one). Write the correct noun in each space.

children   feet   mice   geese   men

One   Many

foot   _____

man   _____

child   _____

mouse   _____

goose   _____

✿ Here are more nouns which change to become many. Write the correct noun in each space.

| teeth | women | oxen | dice |

One   Many

woman   _____

tooth   _____

die   _____

ox   _____

✿ These nouns do not change. Make them many.

sheep   _____

deer   _____

✾ Colour the flower if the noun means many.

✾ Write the word 'one' or 'many' for the underlined noun.

1. The <u>men</u> are in the boat. _____

2. The <u>woman</u> drinks a glass of mauby. _____

❀ **Make the nouns more than one. Write them in the correct spaces.**

foot	woman	man	sheep	
goose	child	tooth	die	mouse

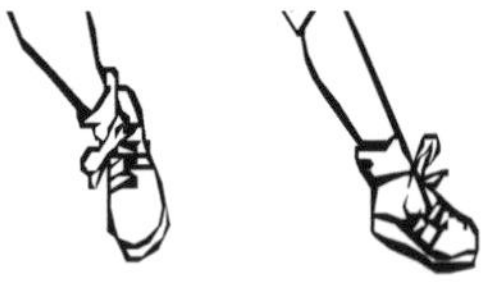

✿ **Make the noun in brackets more than one.**
   Write it in the space.

1. The _____ are digging a well. (man)

2. Are the _____ on the pasture? (sheep)

3. The _____ were in the garden. (woman)

4. She got her _____ cleaned today. (tooth)

5. Many _____ are in the cupboard.(mouse)

6. Some _____ are in the classroom. (child)

7. Her _____ were broken. (foot)

8. They were playing with _____. (die)

❀ **Make the noun in brackets one. Write it in the space.**

1. The _______________ buys a breadfruit. (women)

2. My _______________ has come out. (teeth)

3. A _______________ is in the boat (men)

4. The _______________ plays with the toy. (children)

5. A _______________ is a cube. (dice)

6. Her _______________ is hurting. (feet)

7. A _______________ is in the hole. (mice)

8. The _______________ is eating grass. (sheep)

✤ Make the nouns more than one. Write them in the correct spaces.

glass   tree   match   deer
box   fish   book   lens   chair

   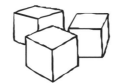   

_____   _____   _____

_____   _____   _____

_____   _____   _____

✼ **Make the nouns many and write them in the correct boxes.**

door   fox   foot   tooth   road   dish

church   truck   man   cane   mouse gas

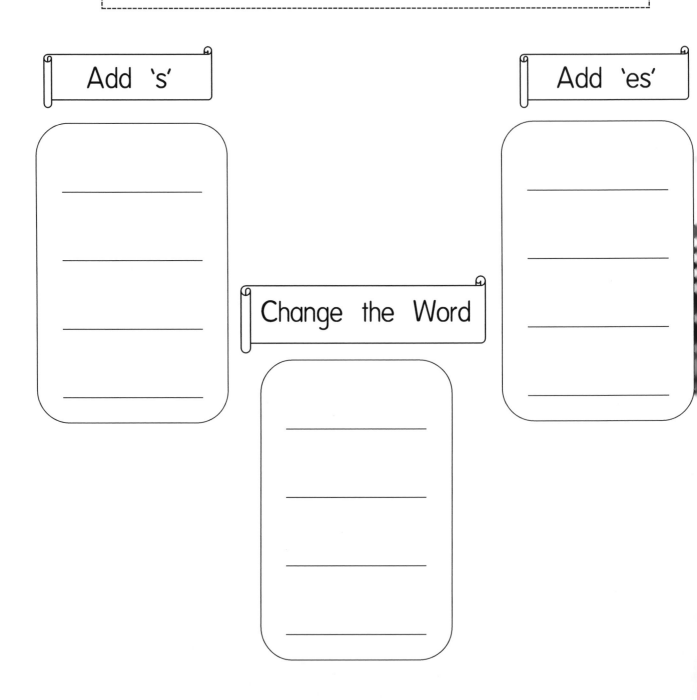

Add 's'

Add 'es'

Change the Word

✿ **Make these nouns many.**

One   **Many**

tooth   _____

chair   _____

die   _____

fox   _____

bus   _____

sheep   _____

bench   _____

woman   _____

Section 4

Verbs

am, is, are

❀ We use the word 'am' when we are speaking or writing about ourselves.

I - - - - -

❀ Write 'am' in the spaces below.

1. I _____ five years old.

2. I _____ in Infants A.

3. I _____ happy to be at school today.

❀ Write 'am' in the spaces.

1. I _____ angry.

2. I _____ afraid.

3. I _____ sad.

❀ We use the word 'is' when we are speaking or writing about one thing, animal, person or place.

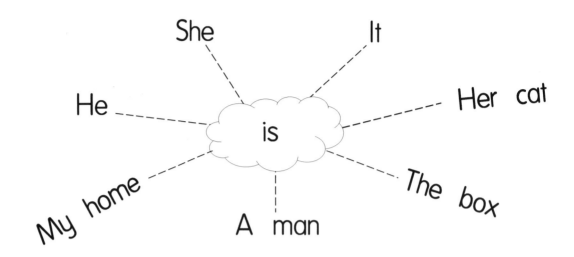

❀ Circle the words which mean one.

girl   birds   cars   wall   it

home   pigs   beds   he   tables

duck   man   she   dogs   hills

❀ Now write the words which you circled on the lines.

_____   _____   _____   _____

_____   _____   _____   _____

✽ In the sentences, circle the word or words which tell us what we are speaking about. Write 'is' in the spaces.

Example: (The bird) <u>is</u> in the tree.

1. A jet _____ in the sky.

2. My book _____ red.

3. The man _____ pulling the net.

4. She _____ playing with her dolls.

5. Ken _____ flying his kite.

6. _____ it a big dog?

7. He _____ going to Three Houses Park.

8. It _____ raining.

✿ We use the word 'are' when we are speaking or writing about more than one thing, animal, person or place.

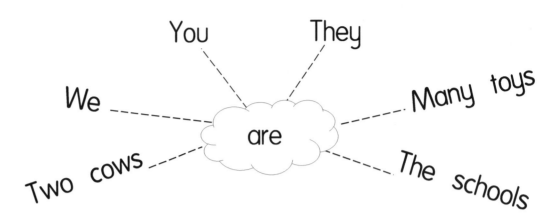

✿ Circle the words which mean more than one.

balls   tree   apple   we   boys

fan   pots   jet   eggs   mats

they   pen   boat   parks   bus

✿ Now write the words which you circled on the lines.

_____   _____   _____   _____

_____   _____   _____   _____

❀ **In the sentences, circle the word or words which tell us what we are speaking about. Write 'are' in the spaces.**

Example: The cups are on the table.

1. My books __________ in my bag.

2. We __________ not going home.

3. The boys __________ picking dunks.

4. Ben and Joe __________ by the sea.

5. The buses __________ on the road.

6. __________ you going to the party?

7. They __________ in the nest.

8. Some men __________ fishing.

✾ **Write the words in the correct boxes to show one or many.**

walls	bus	lunches	boxes
orange	pasture	wishes	fish
children	mice	sun	daddy

One

_____

_____

_____

_____

_____

_____

Many

_____

_____

_____

_____

_____

_____

✤ Complete the tables by putting 'am' 'is' or 'are' in the spaces. We always use the word 'are' with 'you'.

I	
He	
She	
It	
A boy	
My eye	
His book	
Each child	
That car	

We	
You (one)	
You (many)	
They	
The girls	
Your teeth	
Her brushes	
Some boxes	
Those men	

✿ **Match the boxes to the clouds correctly.**

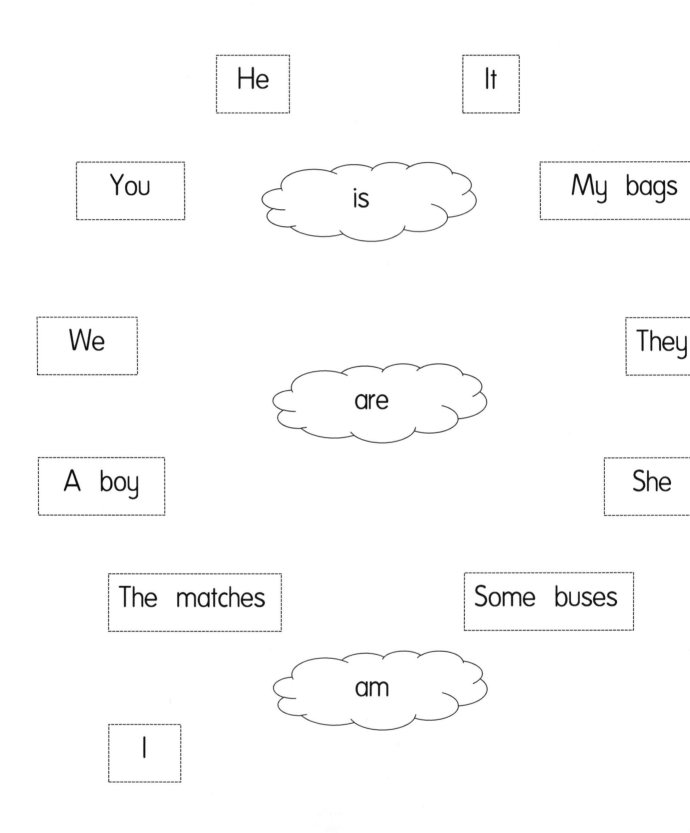

He

It

You

is

My bags

We

They

are

A boy

She

The matches

Some buses

am

I

❀ Write 'is', 'are' or 'am' in the spaces below.

1. A bird __________ on the wall.

2. The children __________ in the park.

3. I __________ not well.

4. __________ it raining?

5. He __________ playing with his dog.

6. We __________ at school.

7. __________ you going with me?

8. She __________ cooking cou-cou and flying fish.

9. They __________ flying their kites.

10. The dresses __________ pretty.

Section 5

Capital Letters

- days of the week
- months of the year
- names of persons
- names of places
- names of animals
- special names

✿ Match the common letter to the capital letter.

a   e   g   r   n   l

G   N   A   L   E   R

✿ Write the capital letters for these common letters.

b _____   d _____   f _____   h _____

i _____   j _____   k _____   m _____

p _____   q _____   t _____   y _____

✿ Write these words in capital letters.

come   down   this

_____   _____   _____

✿ The days of the week always begin with a capital letter. Write these days correctly.

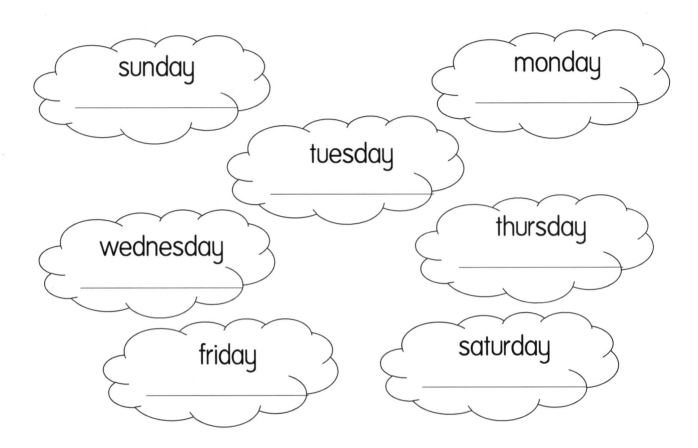

sunday
_____

monday
_____

tuesday
_____

wednesday
_____

thursday
_____

friday
_____

saturday
_____

✿ Write these sentences correctly.

1. She went to church on sunday.

_____

2. Can we go to the beach on friday?

_____

✿ The table shows fruits which some children ate.
Complete the sentences with the days written correctly.

monday	tuesday	wednesday	thursday	friday
mango	tamarinds	watermelon	tomatoes	fig

1. Tom ate tomatoes on _____.

2. Mia had a mango on _____.

3. On _____ Fred ate a fig.

4. On _____ Tammy ate tamarinds.

5. Wendy had watermelon on _____.

✤ The months of the year always begin with a capital letter. Write these months of the year correctly.

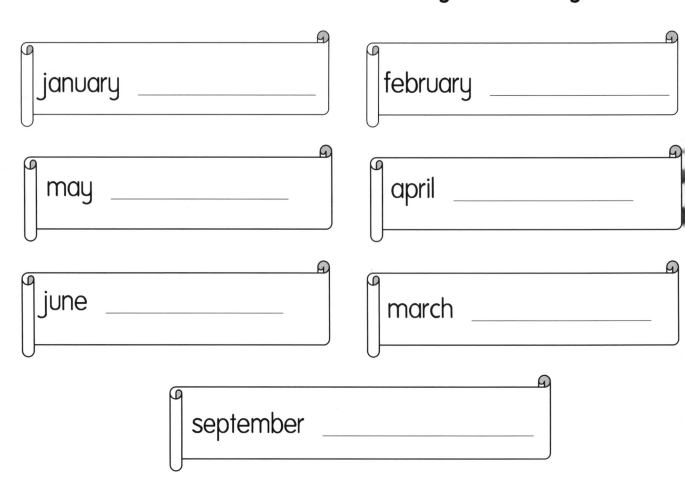

january _____

february _____

may _____

april _____

june _____

march _____

september _____

✤ Write these sentences correctly.

1. My holiday is in july and august.

_____

2. Is her birthday in december?

_____

✿ Write the names of the months correctly in the spaces.

1. Christmas Day is in _____.

   december

2. _____ is the first month of the year.

   january

3. Kadooment day is in _____.

   august

4. _____ 30th is Independence Day.

   november

5. National Heroes Day is in _____.

   april

6. The first of _____ is called Labour Day.

   may

✿ **Always begin the names of persons with a capital letter. Copy the names of these girls correctly.**

jada callender

_____

danielle gibson

_____

✿ **Complete these sentences.**

1. My name is _____

2. My friend's name is _____

3. My teacher's name is _____

4. My games teacher is _____

❀ The table shows things which some children like doing. Complete the sentences with the names written correctly.

cooking	cricket	swimming	football	riding

rhea	joshua	ashlee	nicoli	tiffany

1. ______________________ likes playing cricket.

2. ______________________ enjoys playing football.

3. ______________________ likes swimming.

4. ______________________ likes to ride her bicycle.

5. ______________________ enjoys cooking.

✽ The names of places always begin with a capital letter. Write the missing capital letters for the parishes on the map of Barbados.

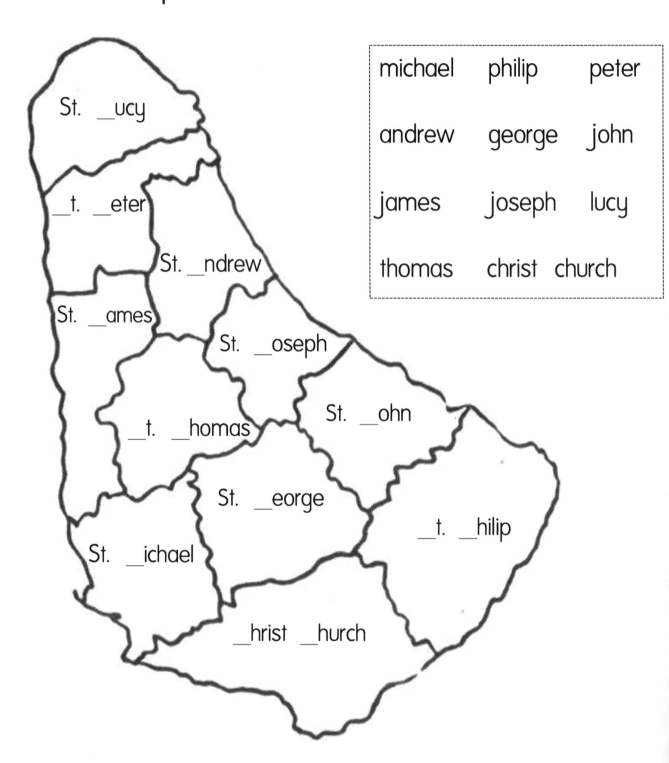

St. __ucy

__t. __eter

St. __ndrew

St. __ames

St. __oseph

__t. __homas

St. __ohn

St. __eorge

__t. __hilip

St. __ichael

__hrist __hurch

michael	philip	peter
andrew	george	john
james	joseph	lucy
thomas	christ	church

✿ **Special names of places always begin with capital letters. Write these sentences correctly.**

1. They went to *oistins* and *bridgetown*.

_____

2. Daddy will take us to *bushy park*.

_____

3. Are they going to *dominica* ?

_____

✿ **Complete these sentences.**

1. My school is in _____

_____

2. I live in _____

_____

❀ Special names of pets always begin with capital letters.

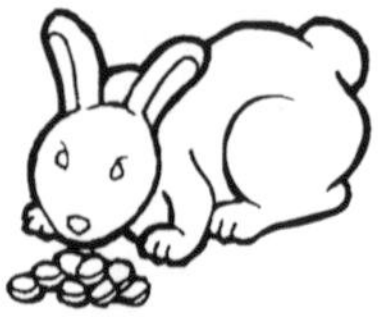

daisy

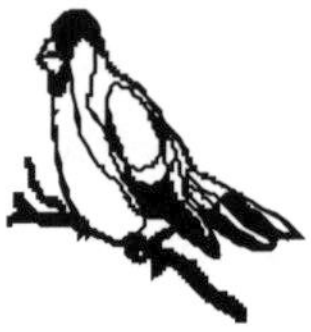

joey

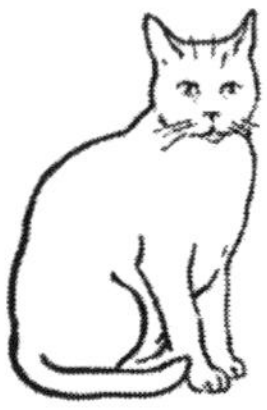

kitty

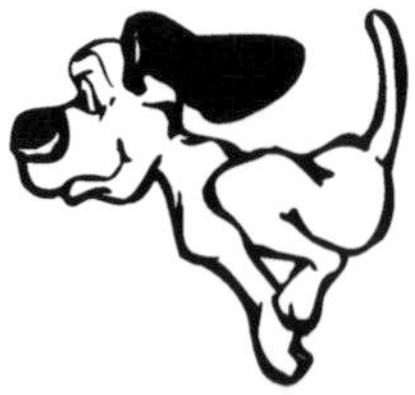

sparky

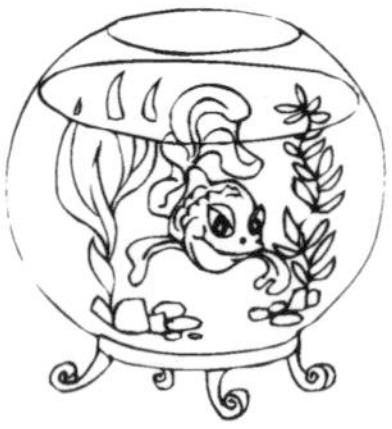

nemo

❀ Complete the sentences with the names written correctly.

1. The fish is ________________.

2. The cat is ________________.

3. The bird is called ________________.

4. The name of the dog is ________________.

5. ________________ is the rabbit.

✿ Special names of things always begin with capital letters.

toyota   samsung   nike   barbie   bico

✿ Complete the sentences with the names written correctly.

1. She has a _____ doll.

2. Daddy drives a _____ car.

3. My cellphone is a _____.

4. I like to eat _____ ice cream.

5. He wears _____ shoes.

✿ **Write these special names correctly.**

miss browne

_____

dr. pinder

_____

mr. edey

_____

---

monday

_____

tuesday

_____

saturday

_____

---

chefette

_____

casa grande

_____

sheraton

_____

---

july

_____

august

_____

october

_____

✿ **Write these sentences correctly.**

1. My cat's name is frisky.

_____

2. She will be six on monday.

_____

3. I sat beside roshanna turney.

_____

4. They live in st. michael.

_____

5. My uncle's birthday is in april.

_____

7. Does your daddy drive a toyota car?

_____

Homework

	Page / Pages		Page / Pages
1		21	
2		22	
3		23	
4		24	
5		25	
6		26	
7		27	
8		28	
9		29	
10		30	
11		31	
12		32	
13		33	
14		34	
15		35	
16		36	
17		37	
18		38	
19		39	
20		40	

Made in the USA
Columbia, SC
23 April 2022

59373244R00052